BAKING YOUR WAY TO THE TOP

How to Start and Grow Your
Own Home-Based Baking
Business

Nicole Bendig-Lamb

For more information, email
nicole@cakebusinessschool.com
Photo credit to Samantha Markey Photography

979-8-88759-213-8 - paperback
979-8-88759-214-5 - ebook

Get Your Free Gift!

To get the best experience with this book, I've found readers who download and use the companion workbook can implement faster and take the next steps needed to start and grow their own cake or baking business.

You can get a copy by visiting:

www.bakingyourwaytothetop.com/resources

Dedication

I would like to dedicate this book to the following person:

Aunt Florence

I remember visiting you when I was just a little girl and you let me help in your restaurant. I watched you cook and create delicious food for your customers, friends, and family with a twinkle in your eye and a smile on your face! You always had a larger-than-life presence and I loved spending time with you. You taught me the art of bringing others joy through food and for that I am eternally grateful.

Table of Contents

Chapter One

My Story: From Cake-tastrophe to Cake-tastic!

I grew up in a small-ish town in Wyoming as the youngest of eight children. One of my favorite activities was being in the kitchen with my mom, aunts, and sisters. During the Christmas holidays, we would gather everyone together to bake sugar cookies, fudge, peppermint bark, peanut brittle, and a variety of sweet treats. As amazing smells filled the air, I always loved being surrounded by flour, sugar, and the happy bustle of everyone together, creating something delicious. At the end of the day, we would make plates and tins filled with the sweet "fruits" of our labor to share as gifts with loved ones and friends.

Between major family holiday baking sprints, many hours of my childhood were spent outside playing in the dirt. What was I doing? Well, I was making mud pies and decorating them with wild cactus flowers from the Wyoming prairie, of course! Once I had my creations complete, I would wash the Wyoming dirt from my little hands, set my Holly Hobby table, and serve my "delicious" creations to my dolls and stuffed animals.

I was also that little girl that you'd see staring in awe at towering wedding cakes at family celebrations. This was not only because I wanted to devour them but because I was completely enthralled by their beauty and detail! I couldn't even imagine how it was possible to create something so gorgeous that would then be cut, served, and eaten.

While many women in my life influenced my love of baking, there was one person in particular—my Aunt Florence. I can best describe her as larger-than-life. She always had a twinkle in her eye and she exuded happiness. When she would visit us, she spent much of her time whipping up incredible food for us in the kitchen. You see, she owned her own restaurant and was the most amazing cook and baker! So much joy was brought to everyone with her amazing meals and desserts. She was the kind of cook who didn't need to measure ingredients. Everything she made smelled and tasted delicious, like her home-made breads, jams, jellies, sauces and pies. Observing her in the kitchen seemed magical to me! She mixed, whisked, sautéd and baked with a genuine smile on her face. When we knew she was coming to visit, my siblings and I would get so excited—and *hungry*!

One summer, when I was about ten years old, I got to visit her, and she let me help out in her restaurant. I would bus and wipe down tables, refill condiment containers, and do other little tasks. But what I remember the most was watching her serve the customers with that ever-present twinkle in her eye, and I could see how happy she made them.

The one pivotal moment for me during that visit, however, was standing in her commercial kitchen and feeling at *home*. As I stood there, smelling mouthwatering steak and baked potatoes, and looking at the cooler filled with delectable pies, one thing caught my eye. There in the midst of the stainless-steel prep tables and shelves was the most beautiful thing I'd ever seen: the giant Hobart commercial mixer. I felt it calling to me, and I was completely mesmerized. At that moment, my little ten-year-old self knew what I was destined for. I wanted—no, I *needed*—to be a baker.

From a young age, I felt there was something magical about creating delicious and beautiful foods, especially sweets.

So, I started baking cakes on my own and trying different things around the kitchen. Attempting different recipes and flavor combinations—some were delicious—most were *OK* at best. But I couldn't keep my mind off of those towering wedding cakes that I was always drawn to like a moth to a flame. I decided that I was not only going to bake a cake but decorate it too!

This first cake was going to be for my oldest sister, Collette. I even planned to bake it and decorate it in her own kitchen. Oh, it was going to be spectacular, I just knew it. Nothing could stop me now! I made the batter, poured it into the pans, and popped them into the oven.

I could hardly contain my excitement as I smelled the amazing aroma wafting from the oven. *Wait a minute*, I thought. *Is something burning? Is that* smoke*?!* As I slowly opened the oven door, the smoke and flames became visible. Holy crap. The cake was *literally* on fire in the oven!

Luckily, my sister had taught me about kitchen fire safety, and I was able to sprinkle baking soda onto the flames, turn the oven off, and wait for the mess I'd made to cool so I could clean it up properly.

I was so upset—crushed, actually. Of course, now I know my mistake was not measuring the batter. Overfilling the pans caused the batter to spill over onto the heating element and catch fire as the cakes were rising. Fortunately for everyone, there was no major damage, except to the cake, *and* my little ego.

You might think that this experience would cause me to give up on my dream. Thankfully, it just made me want to learn more and do better next time. So, with what I like to call the "Three Ps"—persistence, practice, and passion—I kept going. I baked something almost every day after school: cakes, brownies, cookies, etc. I watched reruns of Julia Child on TV with my mom. With the invention of the internet, I started following cake forums and eventually took a few classes. Then came YouTube, and I watched *hours* of tutorials. Over time, I got better.

Fast forward to many years later: I was selected to compete on the Food Network! The production company for a new baking competition show found my website and reached out to ask if I wanted to audition. At first, I assumed it had to be a scam! "Yeah, right," I thought, "there's no way this is real!" To my surprise, however, it turned out to be legitimate. I filmed a three-minute audition video on an old digital camera propped up by a stack of accounting textbooks. Somehow, I managed to edit, upload, and send it to the casting department, even though I had never done anything like that before. After submitting it, I assumed that I would never hear from them again. It was an honor just to be considered. To my surprise though, I was selected to compete! What happened next was a whirlwind that consisted of a flight to Los Angeles, a downtown hotel, and a driver who picked me up every day to take me to the set for filming. I felt like a rock star!

Being on Food Network had been my lifelong dream, and once I had achieved that, I realized I needed a new dream because, you see, even though my ten-year-old self knew she needed to be a baker, I had let a different voice inside my head convince me that I couldn't *really* do that for a living. So instead of being a professional baker, I had spent most of my adult life working as an accountant.

But even though that crappy voice in my head drove my decisions for a long time, that little girl who stood mesmerized in front of the giant commercial mixer was still in there. Her passion was still speaking too! So, I finally listened to her, and together we reached for our new dream—I set out to quit that day job to start my own home-based custom cake business.

You may wonder how I went from a cake on fire in the oven—cake-tastrophe—to having my own successful baking business—cake-tastic? I didn't do it alone. I worked with a cake business coach who helped me break down the steps into manageable pieces. The most important part, though, was helping me see that it was possible.

So now it is my mission to help other aspiring cake artists and bakers achieve their dreams too. I didn't do it alone, and neither should you.

After you read this book, you'll realize too that it *is* possible. You'll learn the steps to make your sweet business dreams come true! This includes everything from the very beginning steps of registering your business name, operating within your local food service and business laws, pricing your products, getting your name out there, and keeping the sales coming, plus more.

That is my hope for you, and I know you can do it. So, tie your apron strings and read on, 'cuz it's time to get going!

Chapter Two

Ten Steps to Start

Cake-tastrophe

In my early twenties, I was working as a part-time administrative assistant in a large corporate office while trying to figure out what I was going to do for my career. If you've ever seen the movie *Office Space*, that was pretty much what this company was like: rows and rows of cubicles, the manager in his short-sleeve shirt and tie slowly sauntering through the maze of desks checking in on the mostly diligent workers while sipping his strong coffee from a "World's Greatest Boss" mug. You get the idea!

Boss's Day was coming up and the company morale squad was trying to come up with ideas to celebrate him. "This is it!" I thought. My chance to show off my mad-baking skills and finally make some cash for one of my creations!

I timidly approached the desk of the assistant office manager with my idea to make a special sheet cake for Boss's Day. To my amazement, she happily agreed! All I needed to do was give her an official invoice, and she'd make sure accounting cut a check for payment. Awesome, right? Since this was my first paid gig as a baker, I had to figure out how to make an invoice, but no big deal, I found a template online to fill in the blanks. Next, I got this great idea to come up with a cute name for my new business—I mean, this was my first paying order, so I wanted to make it count. I decided that my business name was going to be "Nicole's Cakes."

I was stoked when the big day arrived! I showed up with the cake and handed over my invoice. Everyone raved about the delicious dessert. The boss was happy. I got my check. How could it get any better than this?

High on my success, I held the check in hand, ready to cash it in! Then I realized something—oh, crap. I *couldn't* deposit this check. It was payable to "Nicole's Cakes," which, though it was a clever name, didn't really exist. I had no bank account in that name, nor had I officially registered the name as a business. My excitement quickly turned into embarrassment as I did the walk of shame back to the accounting department to confess my mistake. They had to void the original check and reissue one in my personal name, and they weren't too happy about it.

I felt like a little girl whose ice cream cone just got dumped into the dirt. Who did I think I was, trying to have a cake business? Obviously, I wasn't the girl boss I thought I was. It took a long time for me to recover emotionally, but I tell you this story to show that my "mistake" was just one in a long line of learning moments. I can now look back on that day and be proud of past Nicole! She saw and seized an opportunity to take the first step toward her sweet business dream. I just didn't know what I didn't know.

So now that you are ready to start and grow your own baking business, this chapter will outline the steps that you need to take *before* booking your first paying order.

Many people don't start their business because they're held back by two main things: (1) Not believing that it's possible, and (2) Not knowing the steps to begin.

As I mentioned in the previous chapter, I left my boring day as an accountant to pursue my passion for cake full-time. But even though I was an accountant with a business background, I still didn't know where to begin in creating my own home-based cake business. That's where my cake business coach came in to help. She taught me the ten steps to take *before* booking orders. This includes operating legally in your area, bookkeeping, website, business cards/digital promotional material, getting customers, pricing for profit, getting your name out there, giving out samples, having a social media presence, and the final step—try, test, tweak, and repeat.

Step One of *Any* Business: Check the Legality of It

Food Service Regulations

In a baking business, the first thing to look into is the food service licensing/regulations in your area.

Many places now allow certain food items to be sold from a home kitchen. In the United States, this type of licensing is called "Cottage Foods." You will need to check the laws where you live to see if you are able to sell baked goods legally from your home kitchen, which can be accomplished very simply with a quick Google search: "Can I sell food legally from a home kitchen in [insert your home area here]?"

Once you determine if your area allows food to be sold from a home kitchen, you will need to look at the *exact* guidelines. Where I live, our Cottage Food laws allow baked goods to be sold legally from a home kitchen with certain restrictions. For example, we are not allowed to sell any products that require refrigeration—like cheesecakes and fillings that are not shelf-stable—and we are not allowed to sell wholesale. We must also have a business license, complete a food service certification/ safety course, and are required to collect and remit appropriate sales tax.

If you discover that you cannot legally sell from a home kitchen in your area, don't get discouraged! There could be other options for you to pursue. Some examples include renting time in a commissary kitchen, using a church or event center kitchen, or you might be able to find a local small restaurant or café that would allow you to use their kitchen. When I first started my baking business, my state did not yet have Cottage Food laws, so I had to rent time in a bingo hall kitchen. While it was not as convenient as using my home kitchen, it worked out well, and I did this for years until our state opened up to Cottage Food laws.

Tax Identification Number

Another step to operating legally includes getting your tax identification number. If you live in the United States, this can be done for free directly from the Internal Revenue Service website. Note: you should *not* have to pay to get your federal tax ID number with the IRS! Make sure that you go to irs.gov to do this. There are many businesses that will do this for you for a fee, but this is an unnecessary expense. It's very easy to do it yourself directly with the IRS.

If you live outside of the United States, you can do a quick Google search to find out what type of tax steps you need to take in your area. Also please note that it is *your* responsibility to check into your local laws and jurisdictions on your own. This book is meant to be a resource to guide you in the right direction; it is not meant to provide tax advice and is not a substitute for obtaining your own tax professional.

Business Name Registration and Bank Account

You'll also need to register your business name and open a business bank account in that name— remember my epic fail from the beginning of this chapter?

Many people like to choose a fun business name that's catchy and unique. You could operate under your own name, but I recommend having a business name as it's more professional and helps you treat your business like a business and not like an expensive hobby.

If you live in the United States, registering a business name is very easy and is done with your Secretary of State's office. There is usually a nominal fee for this, and you will also have to pay an annual fee to keep your business name in good standing.

Food Safety Certification

I mentioned that in my area, we are required to pass a food safety certification course. The course I completed was online and was not very expensive. This step ensures that you understand food safety for the benefit of your customers and to protect your business as well.

Insurance

The next step in the legality of running a baking business is to make sure that you have food liability insurance protection. This is crucial! You need to make sure that you are protected in the rare event that someone gets sick or injured from your product.

I also highly recommend that you speak to your insurance agent and procure general business liability insurance as well, which protects your business from claims against bodily injury or harm outside of food-related claims. An example of this is if a customer slips and falls on your property while picking up a cake. It can also be a good idea to have an additional layer of protection on your auto insurance to add coverage if you deliver your products.

Sales Tax Licensing

The last part that's crucial for operating legally is to make sure you are collecting and remitting sales tax in your area, if required. This can be a bit complex. For example, in my city, businesses are required to collect and remit sales tax at the state's rate *and* each suburb and county can have different rates that a business must calculate and remit. Also, food products often have their own sales tax rules and regulations, so if you feel overwhelmed, check with your local accountant to help you get set up and make sure that you are collecting the correct amount and filing the reports appropriately.

Step Two: Decide on Your Bookkeeping System

Bookkeeping is definitely not super fun—believe me, I know as a former accountant! But it is vital to your business. It is impossible to know if you are profitable if you don't track your numbers. This is also another way to differentiate yourself as a badass business owner instead of a hobby baker.

You can start off with some easy Excel spreadsheets to track your revenue and expenses. In this book's resource section, I've provided links to a few free templates. Or you can jump right into using an accounting/bookkeeping software such as QuickBooks or Xero.

Step Three: Build a Website

You will also need a website for your baking business so your customers can easily learn more about you.

If you're just starting out and you're on a budget, I would recommend that you start out with a do-it-yourself option.

There are many places where you can get a free or very low-cost website. The advantage to this option is that they normally include templates that you customize yourself with minimal time that will look very nice and professional! Some examples for these are WIX and Squarespace, but I highly recommend BiziChix, which is a great low-cost option, specifically for bakers!

If you have a little more money and you want to go with a higher-end option, you can hire a web designer.

Note: I've included links for all of these recommendations in the book's resources section.

Step Four: Create Promotional Materials

You are going to want business cards or other marketing materials to distribute when you're out and about. Don't forget to include some of these materials with your baking orders so that your customers can market for you!

Your business cards should include your business name and logo, your phone number, your email address, your website, and your social media handles. It is also a good idea to make your card visually appealing! For example, include a photo of one of your creations that matches your logo/branding colors. Or include a nice headshot of yourself in your kitchen holding one of your creations.

An alternative to a traditional business card is post-card-size marketing material that has high-quality pictures of your cakes or desserts along with all of your contact information. I love handing these out at networking events because you can fit more images on a postcard than on a business card, and let's face it, our business is highly visual!

If printed business cards feel too old school for you, consider creating a digital business card. I recently purchased a Popl, which is a small tag placed on the back of your phone that lets you instantly share your social media, payment platforms, and con-tact info just by tapping your phone to any other compatible smartphone. I take this with me when I have a vendor booth at wedding events so that couples can instantly have all of my contact infor-mation, as well as links to my social media without giving them a physical business card.

Step Five: Market Yourself

Now you need to start getting the word out about your new business venture. One of my favorite say-ings is, "You can't sell a secret." If your customers don't know you are open for business, how can they buy from you?

A good place to start is to tell everyone you know that you now have your own baking business and you are taking orders! Chances are you've already been making cakes for friends and family mem-bers, and this won't come as a huge surprise to your biggest fans. So spread the word and tell everyone to help you out.

You should also make announcements on your personal social media to direct customers to find your new business accounts. We'll talk more about more advanced marketing in future chapters, but for now, you'll want to start simple with just spreading the word.

Step Six: Price for Profit

The number one question that I see in cake forums is "How much should I charge for this cake?" I will go into more detail about this in future chapters, including an explanation of how to cost out your creations, what profit margin you should shoot for, and how to add additional up charges for more detailed or custom work. For now, just know that this step is important, and even though you may be scared about pricing and charging for your worth, I'm going to help you through this!

Step Seven: Attend Events

Another great thing to do when you're just starting out is to attend events.

The first summer after I quit my day job, I had a vendor booth at a farmer's market every weekend for about six weeks. I sold cake pops, cookies, brownies, and cupcakes. I had dummy cakes, a portfolio of my work, and I gave out small free samples. This was a great way to let my community know that I had hung out my shingle for business. I also collected names and email addresses to start building my customer database by holding a drawing for a free box of cupcakes in exchange for their information. By the end of the six weeks, I had built my email list up to several hundred potential customers. I also was able to book several custom cake orders right from my vendor booth!

Step Eight: Share Samples

Giving away small free samples to some of my local businesses was another way I was able to successfully spread the word. Most businesses were very happy and welcoming, especially since I came bearing gifts! Who doesn't like free food?

Step Nine: Have a Presence on Social Media

You most likely already have personal accounts on Facebook, Instagram, TikTok, or other platforms, and you will want to have business accounts for all of these as well.

A good rule of thumb is to be most active where your target customers are hanging out. Think about the type of platform that works best for a cake business. In my experience, I have the best luck with Facebook, Instagram, and Pinterest, and while writing this book, TikTok has become a *huge* platform where many cake artists have accounts and share great videos to encourage customers to check out their businesses.

Step Ten: Try, Test, Tweak, Repeat

The tenth step might seem silly—try, test, tweak, and repeat the nine steps above—but you won't know what works for you until you try. I've gone through multiple versions of my own printed marketing materials, with each slight changes to each iteration until I landed on the one that seems to yield the best results.

I encourage you to put a plan in place and only try a few things at a time to avoid being overwhelmed. Also, if you try too many things at once, you won't know which ones work and which ones are not the best use of your time.

Cake-tastic

That covers the ten steps to getting started in your cake business, and yes, they are the same steps I used to quit my day job and achieve my dream of starting my own baking business.

So, check out the resources provided and get going with these ten steps. Then we'll move on to setting your business intentions and goals.

Chapter Three

Setting Your Clear Business Intentions

"To begin with the end in mind means to start with a clear understanding of your destination. It means to know where you're going so that you better understand where you are now and so that the steps you take are always in the right direction." —Stephen R. Covey

Cake-tastrophe

When I first started my own cake business, I thought I had a clear vision of what I wanted it to be, but I really didn't. I knew I wanted to make wedding cakes, but I also thought I could do tons of other things . . . birthday and celebration cakes, cookies, brownies, and pies. I even went into a short stint of making toffee. While I was getting some orders here and there, I really didn't know what direction I was going in. I felt like I was randomly paddling a boat in the middle of a foggy lake. I could see what was right in front of me, but as I paddled in one direction or another, I had no idea what was just out of sight. As you can imagine, feeling scattered and aimless was not very efficient for my time, nor was it profitable. Trying to do too many things that all required different supplies, tools, and processes made it quickly clear to me that there was *no way* I could sustain it all, let alone scale and grow my business without a clear vision of my destination.

So how do you get clear on your intention for your business? I firmly believe that you will be more successful in your business if you focus on the types of cakes or baked goods that light *you* up. You will most likely find that these types of creations are also the ones that you have a natural talent for as well.

Even though I *thought* I knew what I wanted for my business, it took me more self-exploration to really pin it down. In this chapter, I'm going to share with you the exercise that I used to help me gain clarity with this.

Note: you can find this exercise in the supplementary documents at https://bakingyourwaytothetop.com/resources

First, grab a piece of paper, or download the supplementary PDF. Now sit down in a quiet environment with a nice cup of tea, coffee, water, or whatever beverage you enjoy and answer the questions. Know that you'll get the most out of this exercise if you are *completely* honest with yourself! It's a bit like filling out a dating profile. I met my husband on eHarmony, and I believe that we are such a great match for each other because we were both extremely honest when filling out our profiles. So if you want a happy "relationship" with your business and good results, then don't skip or rush through this exercise!

Step One: Answer the following questions keeping in mind your cake or baking business:

1. What makes you happy? What do you love doing?

2. What have been your most enjoyable achievements in your business so far?

3. If you could do, be, or have anything in your business, what would you choose?

4. What would you do if you knew you could not fail?

5. You are given a million dollars. What do you do with it?

6. Who inspires you, and what qualities do they have that you most admire?

Step Two: Take a short break and walk away from your answers. Then, come back and read through your answers and highlight words or phrases that jump out to you. Do you notice common themes?

Write some of the words and phrases that feel important to you.

We're going to use these words and phrases to help you come up with your "Big Picture Dream" for your baking business! I'll break this down further for you in subsequent chapters.

But for now, here's an example: Let's say that some of the common phrases from this exercise include "children's cakes," "making kids happy," "sharing my knowledge," and "having an impact."

These phrases can then be written as this sentence: "My big picture dream is to have a full-time baking business where I can focus on creating cakes specifically for kids and where I can also offer instruction for young aspiring bakers."

Step Three: Look at your big-picture vision and start to reverse engineer it! You now know where you're headed—to Point B—and you obviously know where you currently are—at Point A—so you will need to outline the steps it will take to get you from Point A to Point B.

This is done by breaking it down into tiny manageable chunks. I'll share my journey as an example:

Point A: I was working a full-time, nine-to-five office job in accounting with my home-based cake business as a side-hustle.

Point B: I wanted to quit this job and have a full-time career as a Master Theme Cake Designer.

The end goal was to quit my day job and replace that income with cake orders. While working with my Cake Business Coach, we went through a series of questions to drill it down. Here's what our first planning meeting conversation sounded like:

Coach: What is your biggest obstacle in quitting your day job?

Me: I'm not comfortable quitting my day job unless I have a chunk of money saved up first.

Coach: OK, so how much money would you need to feel comfortable quitting?

Me: I would love to have enough saved up to cover six months of personal bills first.

Coach: How much do you have saved up toward this right now?

Me: None!

Coach: No problem! When would you like to quit your day job?

Me: As soon as possible, but in one year's time sounds doable to me.

Coach: Great! Do you have extra money after each paycheck from your day job?

Me: Yes . . . but not as much as I would like to.

Coach: Are there personal expenses that you can cut back on temporarily to help you meet this goal? Think about how badly you want to have your cake business and let that desire guide you to decide what short-term sacrifices you are willing to make in order to achieve your dream.

Me: I'm sure that I can cut back on some nonessentials and make some better choices to help me with this! I want it so bad!

Coach: Also, are you making sure that you are pricing your side-hustle cakes so that you are making a profit from them? If not, you need to start treating this as a business and not as an expensive hobby. I recommend putting half of your profits into your savings toward your goal. Keep the rest in your side-hustle business to keep it slowly growing as you get close to your goal.

Me: Yes! This is a great idea!

Coach: OK, so here's what you are going to do:

1. Go through your personal finances and cut back on everything that is not a necessity with the goal to put as much from your day-job paycheck away as possible (50 percent if you can!)

2. Do number one for your side-hustle business too

3. Open a savings account specifically for your goal

4. Deposit 50 percent of your profits from your cake side hustle into this account

5. Deposit 50 percent of each day-job paycheck into this account

6. Don't take any money out of this account unless it's an absolute emergency!

7. In one year's time, you should have about eight to ten months' worth of personal bills saved up

8. Quit your day job!

Me: I'm so excited!

Side note: I was so determined that I met my money goal two months early and was able to quit my accounting job sooner than planned.

Hopefully, you noticed from this conversation that we started with the end goal in mind. Then we looked at where I was at the time and broke it into little steps to reach the main goal. It's important to point out that the process she took me through was to re-write my desire as a SMART Goal. This is an acronym for Specific, Measurable, Action-Oriented—sometimes Attainable, Results-based—sometimes Relevant and Timely.

I started with the goal: "I want to quit my day job and replace that income with my own full-time cake business."

This turned into a SMART Goal: "I will save 50 percent of every day-job paycheck *and* 50 percent of my side-hustle cake business profits in a special savings account for the next twelve months so that I will have at least eight to ten months of personal bills covered, and then I will be able to quit my day job and go all in on my full-time cake business."

SMART Goals are a huge part of my success, so I will be talking about them a lot in subsequent chapters. The more specific you can get—really drilling down into what you want—the easier it will be to take it one step at a time.

Cake-tastic

When I did this exercise for myself, I found that the cakes that aligned most with my passion and talents were out-of-the-ordinary, sculpted cakes that didn't look like a cake but instead looked like an everyday object, or themed cakes with lots of realistic elements and details. I love science fiction and horror movies, so many of my cakes have a bit of a crazy twist to them! Even though I still love creating beautiful and classic wedding cakes, I get super jazzed when a couple asks for a uniquely themed design. This exercise also helped redefine how I wanted my website to look. If you check out snarkysweetcakechick.com , you'll see how I was able to really showcase my unique personality and style. Only then was I able to come up with actionable goals and steps to move the needle—like finally having a compass in my foggy little boat instead of floating aimlessly.

In the next chapter, we'll go through filling in a simple business plan to help solidify your SMART Goals into actionable steps.

Chapter Four

Drafting a Business Plan

Cake-tastrophe

When my niece, Jill, was celebrating her sixteenth birthday, naturally I wanted to create something special for her!

This was one of the first multi-tiered cakes I ever made. I decided to have a six-inch round cake on top of a ten-inch round cake with white frosting, piped buttercream swags, and purple royal icing flowers at the meeting points of each of the swags.

What could make this even more special? Sixteen candles, of course! I thought it would be *brilliant* to place ten candles equally distanced along the top of the ten-inch tier and the remaining six candles onto the top tier. Seemed like a great idea at the time, until we lit the candles.

As Jill sat with the cake in front of her and a giant smile on her face, we all stood around singing the best ever off-key family rendition of "Happy Birthday." Right in the middle of the serenade, I saw the royal icing flowers burst into flames and smelled the tell-tale sign of burning sugar. I shouted, "Oh my God! Blow out the candles! Blow out the candles! The cake is on fire!" Jill sat perplexed. "But you're not done singing."

After extinguishing the flames—and my embarrassment—we were able to salvage most of the cake to serve.

So what went wrong here? I had failed to plan out the design first. Instead, I made it up as I went along without thinking of the end in mind.

In the last chapter, we covered your "Big Picture Vision" and talked about rewriting that as a SMART goal . Now you'll start with the end in mind as we continue to chunk down each level in the same process. Like designing a tiered cake—you'll have your sketch of the finished product right at the beginning, so you know where you're headed, but you don't stop there when designing. You need to break that cake into the steps to build it up—the separate elements—the sizes of the tiers, the flavors, the fillings, the frosting or fondant, the embellishments, the supports, etc. Each separate tier and element of a cake is a separate step, and had I followed this with Jill's cake, maybe I wouldn't have set off the smoke alarm.

So let's dig into reverse engineering the steps of your business one at a time, just like you do when you design a tiered cake! You will learn how to break this process down and write SMART goals that fit your current situation but also support your long-term, big-picture goals. By the end of this chapter, you will have an actionable plan that helps you hit that target.

We will start with one more exercise to make this even easier. It's what author Mike Michalowicz calls a "Lifestyle Congruence Evaluation" in his book *Fix This Next*. This is where you will determine what level of revenue your business will need to generate to support the lifestyle that you are *currently* living. In other words, you will analyze what your take-home pay needs to be, and then you'll reverse engineer this back to your top-line sales. Don't set an arbitrary revenue goal! You need to know what you realistically need to make—and do—in your business. Many business owners miss this vital step and don't take the time to do it. Don't make that mistake! It's like shopping for ingredients without your grocery list. If you don't know what you need, then how can you be sure you have everything required to bake your cake?

This may sound hard and mysterious, but it's really pretty simple! Here we go!

Note: a downloadable worksheet is available in the book resources that you can use for this exercise.

Question: How much in cake/baking sales do I need to bring in to support my personal comfort?

Step One: Add up your annual living expenses. This is your comfort level, *not* your dream income—that will come later! What amount will make it so that you're not begging on the street, but you're not a global traveler either? Be truly honest with yourself. What could you do without in your personal life to reduce the initial burden on your cake business?

Look at your personal monthly expenses and categorize them according to the list below. Again, this is just where you are right now! You won't have to live like this forever. These are *temporary* sacrifices that you are willing to live without to meet your goal.

You may not want to do this exercise, and it will most likely make you feel uncomfortable, but trust the process!

Categories

1. Must have/completely necessary. Examples: basic needs like mortgage or rent, food, gas, utilities

2. Nice to have, but not necessary. Examples: streaming services, dining out, subscriptions for entertainment

3. Completely unnecessary. Examples: luxury or splurge items (like a designer handbag)

Step Two: How much revenue must your cake business bring in to support this lifestyle?

To figure this out, you'll determine a percentage of your revenue that you will set aside to pay yourself. Let's start with 35 percent of the deposited revenue to be set aside for your owner's pay. So if you decide that you need $30,000 take-home pay annually to live comfortably, then your cake business will need to generate $85,714 in annual sales.

This has been calculated by taking the necessary take-home pay divided by 35 percent. This percentage is only a starting point; we will discuss this further in the "Profit First" section of the Pricing Chapter later in the book.

Whether you are looking for a full-time income or just extra money as a side-hustle, the math is the same. For example, let's say your cake business is a side-hustle right now and you are looking to make an extra $500 take home per month selling cakes, then you'd do the same math to decide how much per month in revenue you'd need: $1,428.57.

So if your average custom cake price is $200, you'd only need to make seven cakes per month to achieve this! That's only about two custom cakes per week, or perhaps just one wedding!

Note: This process is the *starting* point. You will continue to evaluate on a regular basis to tweak and adjust as needed to meet your goals.

There are many moving parts to finding your sweet spot (pun intended!), and we'll get to them all by the end of the book.

Remember to be patient and don't beat yourself up if you're not where you want to be! What isn't measured can't be improved, so we start here and grow as we go.

Recap of Lifestyle Congruence Evaluation steps:

- Download the worksheet which can be found at https://bakingyourwaytothetop. com/resources

- Calculate your monthly expenses (or the amount you'd like to take home)

- Apply the formula to determine your needed sales revenue

Now you're ready to start your business plan!

As I said previously, what isn't measured can't be improved. If you want a profitable business, you need to be measuring and tracking. And that starts with a business plan. Think of this like a New Year's resolution where we set the intention for the year. A business plan is setting the intention for the business year.

Consider, how much money do you need *and* want to make in the next year? Or, what type of business do you want? It's all connected; your business plan is a working document that you don't write just once and then walk away from. It is constantly evolving as you grow, and it gets changed and updated frequently. Your plan is your map or compass—remember my example of paddling aimlessly around in a boat on a foggy lake?

The process of writing a business plan starts with your intentions for the future, where you are in your business currently, and with looking back. Looking back on the past year, or so far in your business and readjusting your path to stay on track.

Since you have performed the Lifestyle Congruence Evaluation, you should now have an idea of how much revenue you need to generate in your cake business to meet that. Now you will take a look back at prior sales.

Note: If you didn't have a business last year and have no numbers to refer to, don't worry! Just know that your numbers are important in business and you want to be tracking your stats and doing book-keeping regularly to stay on track.

If I ask you, how much did you earn from cakes last year or so far in your business? Do you know the answer? Looking back is as important as looking forward.

How much did you make in the last year in terms of gross sales, and how much in expenses?

When I set my income goals, I start by looking back at the previous year's numbers, which is pow-erful. Without knowing my numbers, how can I move or grow (and by how much) if I don't have a starting point? And how will I know if I reach my goal? I also need to keep my Lifestyle Congruence Evaluation number in mind (this can and should be updated at least twice a year).

For example, if I want to increase my profit by 20 percent, I need to know what profit I made last year, and by end of the year, I will know if I reach that number.

Don't overthink this.

Don't freak out.

If you know the amount, write it down. If you don't know, have a guesstimate.

In gross amount, how much did you earn (IN YOUR BUSINESS) last year?

Just a heads up about this exercise: you may be resistant to it because that means your bookkeeping needs to be up to date. If you don't know your numbers, your profit—or lack thereof—may come as a surprise. It is, however, important—trust me. You are planning on improving your income and that *only* comes from knowing your numbers.

You can download the business plan worksheet included in the book's resources and below are the steps to take for this exercise.

Step One: How much did you make in the last twelve months and what types of orders were there?

Gross sales: the total amount received from customers

Total expenses: the total spent to create these orders

Knowing your income and expenses gives you a starting point. Remember, they can be improved, so don't get all "Debby Downer" on yourself.

What was the number one biggest seller? Now, unless you sell products off the shelf, I understand if this is a little difficult to calculate as each cake order is different, so try finding natural groups or similar sales. Find what type of product, package, or way of selling was the most popular. I recommend looking at your order book to see if there is something similar about the orders, whether it was cupcakes, multi-tiered fondant cakes, wedding cakes, themed party packages, cake pops, or the farmer's market you attended.

For example:

Boxes of twelve cupcakes (you sold about five per week)

Cakes between $100 to $200

Markets

Custom Cake Orders

Step Two: What were your five biggest sellers? (Bonus points if you can list them in order!)

Tip: Notice your biggest seller(s) and think of the eighty-twenty rule. Usually, our biggest seller brings in 80 percent of the income and takes 20 percent of the time. While our little money earners bring in 20 percent of income and take 80 percent of the time. (Hint: this will give you great insight into what to concentrate on this year and what *not* to concentrate on.)

Look back on the last twelve months. What worked? What didn't?

We are talking about what 'worked' in the sense of reaching last year's goals, whether it was increasing your email list, generating more income, creating sales, or having great profit margins.

For example, did you do a Mother's Day promotion that was popular? Or was there a market/festival that had great sales? Did you add an opt-in to your website? Did you write consistent email newsletters? Was there a marketing strategy that worked—email newsletters, connecting with a party coordinator, a giveaway, a deal/promo?

Step Three: Before getting into the big plans and goals, take a step back. What do you want in the next twelve months?

You can refer back to your intentions from the previous chapters for this part. Or this might have changed for you while working on this exercise! Sit with it for a moment and jot down your ideas. This is your dream business!

Examples:

Work [x] number of hours

Increase income (or reduce expenses)

Go on family holidays

Get a new handbag quarterly!

Switch off Sunday (completely off of technology, emails, and cooking)

What do you want the next twelve months to look like?

What do you want the next twelve months to feel like?

What do you want to give yourself in the next twelve months?

Step Four: What are your *big-picture plans?* What big ideas and dreams do you have for yourself and your business?

I am talking about business goals in this instance.

For example, do you want to:

Increase average sale amount

Increase email subscriber numbers

Start your sweet business

Get a business mentor/coach

Get a website or update your website

Earn more money

Increase website hits

Raise prices

Blog regularly

Be fully booked out a month in advance

Now write down all of your big goals!

Are your goals SMART?

Specific

Measurable

Achievable/Action-oriented

Relevant/Results-based

Timely

Be as *Specific* as possible (why, what, when, where, why, how)

Measurable (from and to) by tracking the progress and measuring the outcome.

Achievable (how) by being reasonable enough to be accomplished? Or,

Action-oriented: (what) action will you take to accomplish it?

Relevant (worthwhile) by fitting in to your long term plans? Or,

Results-based (what) results are you looking to achieve?

Timely (when) and include a time limit (hello, sense of urgency!)

Think back on your big-picture goals and let's smarten them up!

Examples:

GOAL: I want more email subscribers.

SMART GOAL: I want to increase from one hundred email subscribers to four hundred by December 31, 20XX.

GOAL: I want to earn more money.

SMART GOAL: I want to increase my net profit from $20,000 to $30,000 for the financial year.

GOAL: I want to earn more money.

SMART GOAL: I want to increase average sales from $150 to $250 and a minimum of three orders per week by June 20XX. I want to be fully booked out (approximately six orders averaging $200) by December 31, 20XX.

GOAL: I want more website hits.

SMART GOAL: I want to increase the average monthly website hits from one thousand to two thousand by December 31, 20XX.

Step Five: Do it.

How are you going to do it? Break it down into mini-tasks (again, make sure they are specific and timely) and use your Lifestyle Congruence Evaluation to determine how many of each product you'd need to sell to meet this.

Example: If you need to make $1,700 in monthly sales, break this into your product sales.

Your average cake price is $150, so you'd need to make eleven cakes per month (or about three cakes per week), etc.

Schedule it in. Then do the work.

Look at your SMART goals. Most people get stuck on the *how*. That is when they usually walk away from their goals and don't really look back. They might start doing the work but don't follow through . . . and why would they?

There are too many unanswered questions. This is why I teach reverse engineering, which is looking at each big business goal and working out the HOW. Then you're able to break it down into mini-tasks and schedule it in.

Then (here is the kicker) you need accountability! Someone who asks you, "What is your goal, and when are you going to do it?" Then having that person follow up and ask, "Is it done?" *That is how to get stuff done.* Accountability! You will get it done because you know someone is going to follow up with you. Note: having someone who can help you stay on track is *huge*! You want to pick someone who is your cheerleader but who will call you out on your BS if you don't keep on top of it (think "tough love").

Now you are completely ready to fill in your first one-page business plan! Yay! All that work you just did was the hard part, so this is going to be a breeze! Download the one-page business plan template in the book's resources at https://bakingyourwayto-thetop.com/resources.

The plan looks like this:

List your three biggest sellers (example: markets, kids' cakes, wedding cakes, other goodies, etc.)

List your three best marketing strategies (example: word of mouth, markets, social media, networking, website, etc.)

List your three top goals for the year

List last month's income vs. this month's income

List last year's income vs. this year's income

List potential income streams plus a breakdown

    For example:

    Kids' cakes = $600

Weddings = $1,500

Markets = $400

Other desserts = $200

TOTAL = $2,700

List Marketing ideas

Idea One = Current Number vs. Target

Idea Two = Current Number vs. Target

Idea Three = Current Number vs. Target

Write down the date you will review this plan. Is it on your calendar?

Write down your accountability partner's name. Schedule a time to check in with them.

So by now, you should have a good starting plan for your baking business, and as the old adage says, "Failing to plan is a plan to fail." So don't fail!

Cake-tastic

Just as I learned the importance of fully planning every step of each cake I design (thanks to setting Jill's cake on fire), I do the same for my cake business. Starting with the end goal in mind and then reverse engineering it step-by-step into manageable bites.

Next up, we'll talk more in-depth about how to price your products . . . for PROFIT!

Chapter Five

Pricing for Profit

Cake-tastrophe

My first paid wedding cake order was one of the most beautiful cakes I've ever made—even to this day. The wedding was to be in a small town in southwestern Nebraska and I agreed to not only create a four-tiered cake for 350 guests but to deliver and set it up, seven hours away from my home in Colorado. I also agreed to stay to cut and serve this massive showpiece.

The design was gorgeous! The bride wanted the cake to be similar to the wedding cake of musicians Jessica Simpson and Nick Lachey (this was in 2004). It was white buttercream with fondant draped swags, plus *three hundred* gumpaste roses, *six hundred* gumpaste leaves, and *nine hundred* gumpaste filler flowers. Oh, and did I mention that I was also six months pregnant with my son?

Since I had only done family wedding cakes at that point and I hadn't officially set up my business yet, I really had *no* idea how much to charge for it.

Because I was so desperate for the order, I agreed to *all* of this for $800 plus reimbursement for my gas! Knowing what I know now that cake alone should have been upwards of $6,000 (even back in 2004).

I came home happy and sad at the same time. I was happy because the cake was stunning, and everyone loved it but sad because I realized that I had actually *lost* money doing it.

This chapter is going to focus on one of the most challenging aspects for most small business owners: pricing your products.

Probably the number one question I see in all the cake forums I follow is "How much should I charge for this cake?" While there are different methods for calculating pricing, I truly believe that many people struggle with pricing not because they don't understand the basic math behind pricing for profit but because they feel guilty, weird, or ashamed charging for their cakes!

Why is this the case? I see this a lot in the cake world but also in all other forms of creative industries with photographers, painters, makeup artists, graphic designers, etc. I think a lot of it has to do with the fact that art is subjective and that creative individuals often pursue their art for the sake of the art itself, for self-expression, and to bring joy to others. So often there's this mindset of "I can't charge for something that I love to do." There is also a perception that, when just starting out, you feel weird about taking money as a "beginner." As a result, many creatives will start out creating for *free* to "build their portfolio." Or they have trouble shifting their mindset from "hobby" to "business."

I also see many cake artists let public opinion dictate their own worth. Have you ever had someone ask you to create a cake, and then when you give them a price quote, they say, "Oh my gosh! That's expensive! It's just a cake!" Oh, how this used to hurt my soul! As if I didn't feel scared enough to quote a price in the first place, this kind of reaction makes it a million times worse! But here's the thing—it's *not* "just a cake." Most of us spend years practicing the craft, perfecting recipes, buying specialty tools, investing in courses, and watching hours of video tutorials to create highly artistic and deliciously edible masterpieces that become the centerpiece of celebrations. Yes, at the end of the day, it gets cut and eaten, but it's not "just a cake."

I finally embraced the fact that the people who do not value my creations are not the right fit for my business, and their opinion of the price does *not* affect the value of my creations. It is also not a reflection of me personally. No one can make you feel bad about your prices unless you allow them to!

So before we start talking about the math behind pricing your cakes, I want to make sure that we address your mindset first.

Here are just a few tips to help remind you that you should and *must* charge your worth!

- You are a business, not an expensive hobby

- If it was easy to create amazing cake designs, then everyone would do it, and they wouldn't need to hire a professional

- Your average customer has *no* idea of the time and skill level that goes into creating a custom cake (Many times, if you kindly educate potential customers, they will see the value over the price tag and you may get the order. If they don't, then be thankful! They don't work for under their value and you shouldn't either)

- It's not "just a cake"—it's an experience, a memory, a showpiece and should be valued as such

- Not everyone can afford you and that's OK!

- By charging appropriately for your products, it allows you to stay in business to serve and have an impact on more customers

Now that we've gotten that out of the way, we can finally dive in and learn more about pricing for profit. The following section will explain the different elements that you need to understand in order to price for profit.

Cost of Goods Sold (COGS), Gross Profit Margin (GPM) and Gross Profit Margin Percentage (GPM%)

Cost of Goods Sold: Cost of Goods Sold (COGS) is the cost of materials and supplies used to produce the products that a business sells. Some specific examples in a baking business include: flour, sugar, eggs, butter, cake boards, support dowels, cake boxes. Notice that this list not only includes the ingredients to bake the cake but also any other tangible things that you use in the final product, like supports, cake boards, dowels, etc.

Gross Profit is your income from selling your product minus your COGS.

Income – COGS = Gross Profit

Here's a baking business example:

Cake Sales: $2,000   (Income)

COGS: $ 700   (Minus ingredients/ supplies)

Gross Profit: $1,300   (Money left over to cover expenses like food liability insurance, business insurance, software subscriptions, gas on delivering, office supplies, and anything else you need to spend to run your business.)

Gross Profit Margin Percentage (GPM%) is defined as a percentage of the sales income that exceeds COGS. It is calculated as: Gross Profit / Gross Income x 100 = GPM%

Let's use the same baking business example:

Cake Sales: $2,000

COGS: $ 700

Gross Profit: $1,300

$1,300 / $2000 x 100 = 65% GPM

What does this mean? For every dollar of cake income, sixty-five cents is profit, while thirty-five cents bought ingredients and supplies to make it. These numbers can be used to help determine the price you should charge for your creations.

While there are other methods of pricing, in this book I will be discussing my preferred method of pricing, which I use in my own home-based baking business.

This method is the Gross Profit Margin Percentage plus Labor Method.

What should your GPM% be? Generally speaking, a good Gross Profit Margin Percentage for a baking business is 65 percent or better for your **base** price to charge. This is the minimum price that you start with to cover ingredients and supplies. We will then add on additional charges for more decorative elements or techniques that take time and a higher skill level.

So from our previous example, our base price is good!

Cake Sales:	$2,000
COGS:	$ 700
Gross Profit:	$1,300

$1,300 / $2000 x 100 = 65% GPM

The formula above will tell you what your GPM% was on prior numbers, but how do you decide what to charge on upcoming orders?

So remember back from basic algebra (who said that you'd never use that in real life?), if you know two of the three variables, you can find the third!

The variables you'll know ahead of time are:

1) Your COGS

2) Your desired Profit Margin Percentage

So with those two pieces of information, you can calculate what the customer price should be by using the following formula:

Total COGS / (1 – Desired GPM%) = Customer Price

Let's say you are getting ready to give a potential customer a cake quote. Here are the steps you would go through to use a GPM% method to price it:

Step One: Total up ALL costs of ingredients and supplies needed to create the cake

Step Two: Decide on your desired GPM% (for a home-based baking business, I recommend at least 65% or higher)

Step Three: Use the formula above to calculate the base price to charge

Step Four: Add up additional up-charges for special details, decorative elements, and techniques

Step Five: Add up-charges to the minimum base price calculated

> Example: Customer requests a two-tiered textured buttercream cake with sugar flowers on the top to feed thirty guests.
>
> **Step One:** Cost of all ingredients and supplies needed to create the cake, filling, frosting & sugar flowers: $49.68
>
> **Step Two:** Desired GPM Percentage = 65% expressed as 0.65 in the formula
>
> **Step Three:** $49.68 / (1 − 0.65) = Minimum Base Price to charge customer

$49.68 / 0.35 = $141.95

Step Four: Add on additional up-charges for textured buttercream technique and three large wired gumpaste flowers and gumpaste filler flowers and greenery

$25 for textured buttercream technique

$45 for large wired gumpaste flowers ($15 each x 3)

$25 for small filler flowers and greenery

Upcharges total: $95

Step Five: Figure out your grand total

$141.95 + $95 = $236.95 (In this example, that works out to be about $7.90 per serving.)

To decide what price you set for the upcharges (buttercream technique and gumpaste arrangement), you can decide how long it will take you to complete them and then multiply the time by a desired hourly rate.

You have wiggle room with this piece of the pricing for sure—it depends on a few factors including your skill level and the going rate in your area (for example, rural areas tend to support lower prices than larger metropolitan areas).

Your individual pricing will vary—you can calculate this by determining an hourly rate for design work and multiply how long an item will take; keep in mind though that your expertise has worth! Just because you can make a sugar flower quickly doesn't mean that you shouldn't charge a premium for it. Remember that you've spent many hours practicing your craft and you've invested money in yourself to learn, so that needs to be considered.

Another note to add: With your book purchase, you have access to my Piece of Cake Pricing Calculator, which is a Google Sheet tool designed specifically to help you with this process! Find the link in the book resources at https://bakingyourwaytothetop. com/resources. Along with the sheet, you'll have access to a video training tutorial that shows how to use the sheet. You'll plug in your ingredients and supply costs for each recipe, enter your desired GPM%, and the sheet will instantly calculate your base price for you! Easy peasy!

Here are some additional tips around pricing:

1) Your potential customers want a quick answer when asking for a cake quote, so don't take forever getting back to them. (Have pre-established minimums that you can quote quickly.)

2) Make sure that you add the words "depending on final details" to your preliminary quotes! Since you are responding quickly,

this lets them know that the final order price may be more, depending on what they ultimately choose.

3) Check out other bakeries' prices in your area. This helps you establish roughly what the going rate is for your town or city. (Don't worry, you will still establish your own prices based on your own margins.)

4) Don't go cheap! You don't want to be known as "the cheap cake lady" because you'll have a hard time raising your prices later—you won't be able to make a profit—and you'll undercut other cake artists. I know you think you have to be cheap to get started, but don't. Just don't.

5) Use three price points when quoting. I call this the "three bears method." It's also known as "good, better, best." You give the top-of-the-line option, a middle-of-the-road, and a budget option. Customers like to have choices. For example, you give the original quote, and then offer a slightly less detailed design, and also maybe an option that is for cupcakes instead of a designed cake.

So now that you've gone through the GPM% plus Labor Pricing Method, I want to give you a brief overview and introduction to the Profit First

Methodology (from the book *Profit First,* by Mike Michalowicz) in the next section.

Introduction to Profit First

Since I was an accountant before becoming a full-time cake designer and cake business coach, you may imagine that bookkeeping, cash flow and accounting concepts really jump out at me! One of the systems that I have been using in my own businesses is the Profit First Methodology. What the heck is that? Well, it is a cash flow management system developed by best-selling business and entrepreneurial author Mike Michalowicz. His mission is to "eradicate entrepreneurial poverty."

In his years of business experience, he's seen time and time again how small business owners fall into the same trap: they feel like they must work twenty-four seven and never take a paycheck themselves, let alone have a profit. Have you ever heard the saying that an entrepreneur is the only person who will quit a forty-hour-per-week paying job to work eighty hours for free? It sounds pretty funny when you put it that way, but it happens a lot!

Because Mike was in that trap himself, and because he wanted to help other business owners avoid this too, he developed this cash flow management system designed to leverage human behaviors rather than change them.

In this section, I'll give you a brief overview of the Profit First System, however, I highly recommend that you grab a copy of the book, *Profit First* (bonus: he narrates it himself and give tons of extra stories and resources in the audio format of the book—he's also hilarious and entertaining!). Note: this chapter is not intended to be a substitute for reading the book *Profit First* and/or working with a Certified Profit First Professional but is instead meant to introduce you to this method.

Basic Principle of Profit First: Instead of waiting to pay yourself as the owner *last*, you will allocate a portion of your income and prioritize your owner's pay and profit *first* (hence the name), before covering your business expenses. You will also allocate a percentage of your income to set aside funds for taxes and then your operating expenses. This process will force you to cut or control expenses if there isn't enough to properly allocate. When implementing this system, you open different bank accounts for different purposes to help you properly and regularly set aside funds and use them *only* for their intended purpose, thus removing the temptation that most humans have when we are presented with one big "serving platter."

Now that you know what it is … let me tell you what it *isn't*. Profit First is not a substitute for traditional accounting and bookkeeping in your business but is instead a cash flow management process that you will use in tandem with accounting to help run a fiscally healthy business. You will still need to keep a proper set of "books" for your accountant to prepare your income taxes and to have if you need to apply for any kind of financing or loans for your business.

Let's dive just a bit deeper into the basic concepts of bookkeeping. As I mentioned, you will still have a "set of books" for your business, which basically means all of your revenue, expenses, assets, and liabilities will be tracked in some form of bookkeeping software (common ones include QuickBooks or Xero) or even by using spreadsheets for very small businesses (like Microsoft Excel or Google Sheets). I recommend using accounting software like QuickBooks because it will automatically generate the main financial statements that your accountant will need. These include the Balance Sheet, Profit & Loss (also known as the Income Statement), and a Statement of Cash Flows.

I don't want to overwhelm you with these accounting terms, however, as a business owner, you should at least have an understanding of these terms and what they indicate for the health of your business. Even if you don't do your own bookkeeping, it's important to know and understand what you're looking at!

Here are basic definitions of these terms so that you understand:

Balance Sheet: One of the main financial statements which includes a business's assets, liabilities, equity/capital, total debt, etc. at a given point in time (like a snapshot of the financial position of the company).

Assets: These are resources or things that the company owns. Examples are bank accounts, equipment, and accounts receivable (money owed to the company).

Liabilities: These are debts or obligations that the company owes. Examples are credit card balances, loans, or sales taxes collected.

Equity: This represents the company owner's stake in the business and is calculated by the total assets minus the total liabilities.

Profit and Loss (aka Income Statement): Also one of the main financial statements of a business which summarizes the revenue, cost of goods sold, and expenses during a specific time period.

Revenue: This is the total income produced by the business (for example: the money you bring in from your cake sales).

Cost of Goods Sold: The cost of materials and supplies used to produce the products that a business sells. Some specific examples in a baking business include flour, sugar, eggs, butter, cake boards, support dowels, cake boxes.

Expenses: Expenses are defined as the cost of operations that your business spends in order to generate revenue (examples include rent/utilities, business phone, insurance, bank fees, dues for networking or professional organizations, etc.). As explained in the previous chapter, this is not the same as Cost of Goods Sold.

Cake-tastic

Knowing my numbers has helped me develop a proven pricing structure that I know keeps my business running at a profit. Revisiting this frequently helps me control costs and gives me the peace of mind that I'm being fairly compensated for my talents. I also now have the confidence to counter the "that's too expensive" argument from potential customers, and I take that opportunity to educate them on why custom artisan cakes are worth every penny.

Now that you have a basic understanding of pricing, profit and financial statements, your next step is to jump into marketing your business!

Chapter Six

Marketing

"Marketing is really just about sharing your pas-sion." —Michael Hyatt, New York Times Best-selling Author

Cake-tastrophe

Early in my cake business, I didn't want to tell anyone about my offerings. I didn't want to seem "pushy" or to be a "bother." But then I would be upset when I didn't get any orders. What sense does that make, you might ask? How are my potential customers supposed to know I'm open for business if I don't tell them? The answer is they couldn't pos-sibly know.

As I slowly got better about this, I would *try* to market myself by telling people, "I do cakes." But because I lacked the confidence to even talk about my creations, most people would brush me off and say, "Oh, that's nice." The end.

Another huge mistake I made was feeling like I had to say "yes" to every request. I would agree to every single order whether I wanted to do it or not. I felt like I should. The best example of this is that I personally don't do special diet desserts, but I kept getting asked, "Do you do gluten-free? Do you do organic? Do you do vegan?" And even though I really didn't, I would say yes because I felt like I needed to, and I believed that if I said no, I would never have any customers.

Now I feel bad about taking those types of orders because I'll be honest with you, I am *terrible* at making gluten-free desserts! Seriously.

So in this chapter, I will focus on all things marketing so you don't have to repeat my mistakes.

What is marketing, anyway? Simply put, marketing is sharing how you can help others solve their problems with your products or solutions.

I know you might be wondering if a customer's need for a cake is really a "problem." Sure it is! The kinds of cakes and baked goods that we do as cake artists and skilled bakers are usually not the kinds of things that just everyone knows how to—or even wants to—make themselves. I say it all the time: "If it was super easy, then everyone would do it." You help by making edible pieces of art. You help by saving time. You help by saving frustration—hello, cake pops! You help by being part of a gorgeous event.

Let me put it another way—most customers who order custom or specialty cakes and desserts have many other tasks on their schedule and each task they are responsible for needs to be given time and thought before getting crossed off their list. Sounds like a problem to me, and your mad cake skills are the solution!

Here are some key thoughts before you begin developing your own marketing plan:

There are hundreds of marketing strategies and ways to market your business. Choosing which marketing strategies comes down to you—your preference, personality, your skill set, and what works for you in your business. A strategy that works for me might not work for you. Check out the list of "100 Marketing Tips" in the book's resources section for ideas and suggestions to get the ball rolling.

Remember, whether you have tried it before or not, when you hear the voice inside your head say, "It doesn't work," turn that around and ask yourself "How will it work for me?" Be open to exploring options for different marketing ideas, rather than instantly dismissing them.

The idea is to start laying marketing strategies, like foundational building blocks. There is no one magic marketing tactic that is going to get you a million bucks. But multiple marketing and layered strategies will get results.

In this marketing plan, you'll start with a selection then *try, test, tweak, and repeat* .

The only way to know whether a marketing strategy is effective or not is to judge the results (sales) by evaluating the data and sales figures. Then implement additional marketing tactics brick by brick.

In just a bit, I'll share the step-by-step marketing plan that I personally use, which you can download the template for in the book's resources. But before you dive into the plan itself, let's talk about your mindset for finding your perfect product and your perfect customer.

My mindset starting out:

As I mentioned at the beginning of this chapter, when I first started selling cakes instead of making them as a hobby, I was so nervous about the whole marketing/sales process. I didn't want to seem pushy or sales-y, and I didn't want to "bother" people. But here's the thing: you can't sell a secret! If no one knows you make awesome desserts, how can they buy them from you? This was more of a mindset issue for me. I felt weird about marketing my cake business because I didn't want to seem like a cheesy used car salesman.

I also had no idea *how* to market. Partly because I'd never done it before, and partly because I had a mental block about it. But again, you can reframe your outlook to see that you aren't being pushy at all—you're offering a solution! And if you are a good fit for the customer (and vice versa), then it won't feel awkward at all.

I know this can seem uncomfortable or even scary! Besides reframing my mindset to recognize that I was simply sharing a possible solution for potential customers, one of the biggest "ah-ha" moments I had was when someone told me to not be attached to the outcome.

What does this mean, exactly? Don't focus on "making the sale" or "closing the deal." Instead, just share the information in a natural way. You will feel more at ease and so will your customers! It is also life-changing to realize that not every customer or cake order is a good fit for every baker! Don't take it personally if you don't get every order. It's OK to not get every order. Orders that I don't get clear space for me to take orders that are a better fit for me or that I'm more passionate about. I'm also a huge believer in an abundance mindset. There is plenty of business out there for everyone and taking orders that aren't a good fit for you will cause frustration and potential burnout. Plus, think about the baker who would be a better fit for that customer (again, abundance mindset!).

So how do you ensure that you're a good fit for the customers to whom you're marketing? Not only do you need to understand and feel confident about marketing, but you also need to practice what is called *intentional* or *targeted* marketing. This process involves getting clear on what products are in your zone of genius then honing in on the right customers who would want them and finding out where they are hanging out so you can share your solution to their problem!

Again, I want to remind you how I used to use the "shotgun" marketing approach. I wasn't clear with myself on what specific kinds of products I was going to offer—I thought the best thing was to offer everything to everyone! Seriously, as I mentioned in a previous chapter, my menu had everything from all occasions of cakes, decorated cookies, muffins, breads, cupcakes, truffles, candies, and I even decided at one point to offer homemade toffee. Then I would just try all kinds of marketing all at once—like throwing spaghetti at the wall and seeing which noodles stuck.

To be honest, I had no idea what I was doing, and I just ended up confusing my customers and running myself ragged. I'm not saying that you can only offer one menu item, but I want to stress that having a focus on one or only a few products at a time when you're first starting out will save you exhaustion and confusion.

I want to share another concept from author Mike Michalowicz, whom I mentioned in the Pricing for Profit chapter. In another of his books, *The Pumpkin Plan*, he shares his expertise on not just finding customers but finding the *best* customers who are a great fit for you. He says, "More is not better. Better is better." I absolutely love that concept, and it resonated with me so much at the time since I had been feeling like I needed to say yes to everything and was scared to say no to orders because I was afraid of pushing away business. It became clear to me after reading Mike Michalowicz's books that it was actually smarter to only sell to the best customers for my niche.

So if you've been doing cakes for a while and you've just been saying yes to absolutely everyone, I'm here to tell you that you don't have to—in fact you *shouldn't*.

Wouldn't it be great if you knew that you were only working with the best customers for you? The ones who appreciate what you do and what you're passionate about?

In addition to finding your best customer, you also need to find out what your best product is. What do you love to do? What are you passionate about? Your perfect product is the thing that hits the "sweet spot" between what you absolutely *love* creating and what you have a natural talent for!

I talked about the concepts from *The Pumpkin Plan* and how straying from what you love doing in your business can limit your success (and quite frankly, burn you out!). Just because you can do something doesn't mean that you should. My previous example of how I used to say yes to every order type (including special diet cakes) because I thought that if I said no, I'd never have any customers. What I didn't realize was that if I loaded my schedule up with every order around, then I wouldn't have the time to dedicate myself to the orders or designs that I am really amazing at. Saying yes to the wrong types of orders is doing a disservice to my customers as well as to my own business.

If we all instead focused on the one thing (or few things) that we both (1) love to create and (2) are *great* at, can you see how that really serves your customers better?

Now find your perfect product. Download the worksheet from the book's resources section, compare your favorite types of cakes to make that you identified in the "Intentions" chapter with your best sellers from the "Planning" chapter—do any of these intersect? There will also be a set of questions that you can ask yourself to help define what your best product is.

List to Compare: Your Favorite Past Orders vs. Your Top Sellers

Question to Ask Yourself:

Thinking back on past orders or cakes you've made, do you ever think, "Yay! I LOVE getting orders for cakes like these!" What specifically do you like about certain types of orders? Is it the challenge? Is it the way you feel about the finished product? Is it the reaction you get from the customers? Jot down some ideas.

How about the reaction, "Ugh ... I *hate* these kinds of requests!" Again, what specifically is it about these orders that you don't like? Is it that you don't feel passionate about them? Do you feel like it's just not your forte? Do you feel like someone else would enjoy it more? Jot down your thoughts.

Putting it all together:

Now that you've listed your favorites, compared them to your best sellers, and gotten really specific about what it is that lights you up (or sucks your energy), you should be able to write a sentence or paragraph that clearly describes *your* perfect product!

Below is my example to help guide you:

I love getting orders for science fiction or fantasy sculpted cakes. I love the challenge of figuring out how to pull them off, and I *love* the surprise and happiness that they bring my customers! I don't enjoy orders for special diet cakes as I'm really not good at them, and I don't feel like the final product is up to my quality standards. I feel as though there are so many other bakers who are better (and more passionate about making them) than I am. Therefore, my perfect products are unique sculpted cakes in fondant and other 3D edible mediums where I can focus my passion on recreating awe-inspiring designs in sci-fi, fantasy, horror, or food realism. These are usually milestone birthday cakes, groom's cakes, or retirement cakes.

Now write your perfect product description on the worksheet.

Next, we'll move to Targeted Marketing. By definition, Targeted Marketing is identifying customers who are likely to buy your products or services, then promoting directly to that audience of customers, as described in the steps below.

To Whom Should You Sell? Understanding & Identifying The Perfect Customer For Your Baking Business

Why shouldn't you sell to just anyone? Just as you have identified what goodies are your best products to sell because you are amazing at creating them and you *love* to do so, now it's important to match that with the best customers who will appreciate them the most!

Why not just sell to whoever will buy? You could do this (and many of us have), but it's so much better for your business (and quite frankly, for your mental health!) to find the best customers who align with your business principles, values, and goals.

Why? For several reasons:

• You could have the best cakes in the world but if you're trying to sell to the wrong person, you'll never hit your sales goals.

• You may find yourself compromising your business objectives to try and please everyone.

• When you attract customers who are happy to pay what you need to charge and they appreciate your craft, they will be your ambassadors to spread the word to attract even more of the best customers!

How do you know who your perfect customer is? The process is described here:

1. Identify the segment & name of your ideal customer. Example: If you've decided that you want to focus on creating mostly children's celebration cakes, then the customer segment is most likely going to be the

children's parents. You'll personify this further by giving the parent a name: "Maggie
the Mom."

2. Fill in the demographics/interests. You'll
    want to be very specific to make them feel
    as real as possible to you (which is why we
    have given them a name). We want them to
    come to life for you!

    Examples:

    • Age

    • Gender

    • Marital status

    • Number of children

    • Age of children

    • Location

    • Occupation

    • Quote that sums up their feelings related
    to their problem/goal most closely related
    to your product

    • Brands or influencers they follow or
    engage with

    • Annual income

    • Level of education

• Where they get information (books, blogs, forums, events, etc.)

3. Know their frustrations and fears. You'll list what's relevant to your offers, so following our example of children's celebration cakes, maybe the parents are concerned that they won't be able to find a cake to match their child's favorite teddy bear, or maybe they feel overwhelmed and worried that they will have to bake and decorate a cake themselves, etc.

4. Understand their desires and aspirations. You've thought about their worries, now think about what they envision for their event!

Examples:

• What do they want for themselves?

• What do they aspire to be/have?

• What do they want for the people around them? (Family, friends, coworkers, etc.)

• What goals have they set for themselves?

• What values do they hold dear?

• What are their secret desires?

Try to really "get in their heads" and think about what they really are looking for!

5. Identify their purchase drivers. Now you know their problems and goals, let's figure out why this customer would buy. What things are most important to them?

    • Must-have elements of their dessert

    • Expectations of service

    • Quality expectations

    • Anything that might be a deal-breaker?

    • What could be their common objections?

    • Any other people that will be involved in the decision?

Download the worksheet from the book's resource page and fill in your ideal customer's persona and attributes; then we'll be able to find where they are hanging out so you can connect with and attract them!

Tips to help you figure this out:

•   If you get stuck, doing some simple searches on Google, Facebook, Pinterest, or Instagram can really help! You can type in a search for your products and see what types of clues pop up in the searches.

•   Even searching your competitors can help give you some insight into your potential customers.

• Reading customer reviews is also super insightful!

• Another great resource is to think about any previous customers you have served whom really enjoyed working with. What were some of their characteristics that made them resonate with you?

Here are a few examples and tips to help you find your perfect customers:

Your perfect product is a wedding cake and your perfect customer is a first-time bride.

She's reading local bridal publications (online & print), attending bridal expos, and asking other brides in Facebook groups where they went for their wedding vendors.

You can: Connect with other wedding industry professionals and establish a referral relationship (wedding planners, venues, caterers, florists, photographers, videographers, bridal gown and tux shops, etc.). Another way that you can forge connections is by having a vendor booth at a bridal expo and holding a drawing to win a complimentary box of cupcakes for a shower to collect her name, phone number, email, wedding date, and if she's met with any other cake vendors. Become a preferred vendor with a wedding or event venue. Advertise in your local bridal publications.

Your perfect product is children's birthday cakes and your perfect customer is a mom of elementary-age kids.

She's hanging out at school events and at school pickup and drop-off. She can also be found at soccer practice and dance recitals.

You can: Advertise in the school newsletters, have a vendor booth at school craft shows, have a Facebook business page and join mom groups that allow promotional posts, and connect with other vendors and businesses who cater to children's parties (martial arts studios, kids' party centers, etc).

The basic idea is that if you know your customer, then you should be able to figure out where to find them and come up with ways to connect!

Once you wrap your brain around this concept, marketing should be a piece of cake (pun intended).

Now that you've gone through the exercises to determine what your perfect product is and who your perfect customer is, it's time to just start!

As with anything, sometimes the hardest part is getting started. There are many reasons for this, but one of the main roadblocks is simply not knowing where to start. That's why having a plan to help guide you is essential.

Another roadblock is fear. Two of my absolute favorite sayings around fear are:

- "If you want something you've never had, you must be willing to do something you've never done," and

- "Growth and change happen outside of your comfort zone."

Another pitfall that many bakers experience is wanting their marketing to be perfect. Believe me, I totally get this! By nature, we tend to be perfectionists (think about all the detail you pour into your cakes!). But don't let perfection be the enemy of progress! Why? I'll let you in on a little secret: there is no such thing as perfect. There is, however, good enough. You'll have much better results if you act and move forward with a plan. Even if that plan doesn't go exactly as you'd hoped, this is an excellent learning opportunity as opposed to not acting because it's not "perfect."

Now let's get to the actual marketing plan. You can download the marketing plan template from the book's resources.

As you put together your marketing plan, I will ask you to make the following commitments:

1. Make a commitment to market consistently. If you do it inconsistently, then you will have inconsistent results. If you don't market at all, you'll get zero results. Effort in equals results out. Set aside time DAILY to market your business and get sales. Make this a priority.

2. Instead of saying "This doesn't work for me," say *How* can this work for me?" Flip your mindset. I promise if you think it doesn't work, then it won't.

Key Elements and Steps To Your Marketing Plan:

Select three to five marketing strategies and commit to implementing these. Set your objectives in the form of SMART Goals (Specific, Measurable, Action-oriented, Results-based, and Time-based). Set your marketing schedule: daily, weekly, monthly (consistency is key!). Evaluate your results, then tweak and repeat (or select new strategies).

Step One: Select Your Strategies (three to five)

Below is a list of some top strategies that are tried and true for baking businesses (also refer to the "One Hundred Marketing Tips and Strategies" PDF in the book resources for additional options).

- M ake sure you have a website. If you don't have a website yet decide if this is something you feel comfortable creating yourself or get someone else to do it.

- Have a Facebook business page. Post at least three times per week. Share these posts from your Facebook business page to your personal page. Join Facebook groups and post once a week into the Facebook group.

- Vouchers. Hand out fifty to one hundred. Print off your vouchers, have them on hand to give to friends and family, at hair salons, and even people you strike up conversations with in the grocery store!

- Samples. Take samples (I suggest mini cupcakes) along with vouchers into shops, salons, clothing stores, your accountant, and offices.

- Markets. Research and book into at least one market. It could be a farmers' market, show, expo, festival, or event.

- Create a monthly birthday register for sending emails to book cake orders for upcoming parties.

- Send weekly email newsletters. This can be accomplished through an email service provider (I use and recommend ConvertKit.)

- Network with wedding planners, party coordinators, wedding reception venues, photographers, etc.

Step Two: Set Your Objectives as SMART Goals

Any time that you are spending time, energy, and money, you need to have a very clear result that you wish to achieve.

Example One: From the Monthly Birthday Register, I want ten birthday cake orders booked by the end of June. This will be accomplished by sending emails twice a month with weekly follow-up calls.

Example Two: Approach smash cake photographers. Create a set price or set guidelines in which the customer can order when they place an order with the photographer. Work with the photographer to create a suitable digital image or flyer for advertising. Make sure to advertise three times per month on your Facebook page. Make sure to add a flyer to the top of each cake box geared toward a kid's party. You will set an objective for *each* marketing strategy that you picked from Step One.

Step Three: Set Up Your Marketing Schedule

Example:

Daily: One hour of marketing activities:

• Post in Facebook groups

• Reach out to other event industry professionals to discuss referring to each other

• Reach out to past customers for feedback and offer them a quote for upcoming events

Weekly:

• Follow up on quotes

• Schedule Facebook business posts

• Farmers market/expo/show/event networking

Monthly:

• Send out birthday register emails

• Sound out your monthly email newsletter

Steps Four and Five: Evaluate Your Results, then Tweak and Repeat

How do you know if your marketing is working? ROI (Return On Investment)—you need to check whether the money you invested into your marketing strategy is *directly* resulting in a profit.

Example: You spent thirty dollars on printing discount gift vouchers to hand out at your local Babies & Kids Market and you found that this resulted in $180 worth of orders being placed.

Another way to evaluate your results is by analyzing your sales numbers. This is more specific to your overall marketing plan, rather than individual marketing strategies. You can tell if your sales numbers have increased.

Example: last financial year you earned $26,000, and this financial year you earned $38,000.

Customer Response/Survey: Ask your customers where they saw your name and why they decided to place an order with you. Collect this information over a certain period of time and review it. For example, after each order is complete, send a customer survey with two questions: (1) How satisfied were you with the services? (2) Where did you hear about our business? Because you set clear and measurable objectives/goals in Step 2, this step should be fairly easy to perform.

Looking at the SMART goal you set for each strategy and comparing it to your results, you should be able to answer the following questions:

- Did I fully meet each part of my goals? If not, did I meet any part?

- Which strategies worked?

- Which strategies didn't work?

- For strategies that partially worked, what can I tweak to try again for better results?

- Are there any strategies that didn't work at all that I need to scrap?

- What new strategies will I choose to replace that didn't yield any results?

NOTE: Remember that some strategies may need a longer time to see results than others. This is why you need to evaluate on a weekly basis so that you can keep an eye on your progress.

Now, take all of the above information and fill in your own Marketing Plan from the template included in the book's resources at https://bakingyourwaytothetop.com/resources.

As a reminder, this is never a "one and done" process! This is a process that you will try, test, tweak, and repeat many times over as you develop your business.

Sales Language: **How to hone your sales language so you can sell without sounding cheesy, pushy, or awkward.**

In this last section about marketing, I'd like to share information about how important your sales language can be when engaging with a new potential customer.

Think about a time when you were looking to buy something, and you were approached by a pushy salesperson. How did it make you feel? I can say that when I'm in this situation, I am instantly put off. I don't like this style of selling because it makes me feel as though the salesperson doesn't really care about me as a customer but only cares about closing the deal and making the money.

It also feels very predatory and opportunistic. I'm very put off by fear-based selling, like the whole FOMO scenario, aka the fear of missing out. I find this technique dishonest and unethical. I was once told that I should tell prospective wedding cake clients that I had another party interested in their wedding date (even if this wasn't true), and that if they didn't book with me right on the spot, they could miss out! I am very uncomfortable with this technique. I do not believe in being dishonest with prospective customers, or with anyone for that matter, because it is against my business ethics and code of conduct.

So how can we sell without falling into these common traps? The first thing to think about is that it is not about you as the business owner, but instead, it should be about how you can solve their problem.

Be confident and knowledgeable but not arrogant. Be honest (no BS!). Highlight the value of what you can provide and what positive impact it will have on them. Share what makes you and your cakes different.

Use descriptive phrases to showcase what you offer! Work on your "elevator pitch." As I mentioned earlier, I used to say, "I do cakes," but now when people ask what I do, I say, "I create memories for my clients as a Master Cake Designer."

Everyone knows what a cake is, but not everyone knows what *your* cakes are like! Changing your sales language will open more interest and emotion and can lead to a conversation.

You can even change your title. Instead of saying you are a "Cake Decorator," think about calling yourself something else: (Master) Cake Designer, Sugar Artist, Cake Artist, Cake Magician, Dessert Goddess, etc. You get the idea! Get creative!

Don't forget to make sure that you are attracting the right customer base for your business.

How do you tell who your best customers are?

- They are willing to pay a premium for your product.

- They are a joy to work with.

- They don't hold it against you if you make a mistake and may even participate in the resolution.

I also recommend that you do NOT become emotionally attached to the outcome. If it's a good fit and they're willing to pay what you're worth, it will work out. If it's not a good fit, no amount of pushy, cheesy, fear-based tactics will ever make it a good experience for either you or the customer.

Cake-tastic

Now that I've embraced my niche, my perfect customer, and have gained the confidence to truly share how my cakes help my customers, I no longer shy away from marketing. I can truly say that it doesn't feel like marketing at all. It now feels relaxed and natural, and the best part is that I'm booked up!

In the next chapter, we'll talk about customer service tips and tricks to make sales and keep them coming!

Chapter Seven

Customer Service

"Your most unhappy customers are your greatest source of learning." —Bill Gates

Cake-tastrophe

A few years into my cake business, I was so excited to be getting more wedding orders. I had a bridal couple who originally ordered a smaller wedding cake with the addition of a novelty groom's cake. We had agreed on all the details, and as the big day approached, they reached out and decided not to have the groom's cake after all. "No problem!" I assured them. I made a note to myself and then didn't really give it another thought. The week of the wedding arrived, and as is my usual process, I pulled out my notes to bake and prepare the cake. No groom's cake, check. Bridal cake with gumpaste flowers, check.

I had been preparing the gumpaste flowers ahead of time and was feeling awesome about this order!

The day came, and I loaded up my gorgeous cake and drove to the venue for delivery and setup. I walked in with my creation and found the cake table. All set! Nothing to worry about!

I left the venue and drove back home, basking in my accomplishment.

But then—*ring, ring!* Who could be calling me right now? *Oh God, it's the venue*, I thought. The day-of coordinator was on the phone to tell me that the mother of the bride was *livid*.

"What's wrong?" I timidly asked. "She says that she paid $700 for a cake to feed one-hundred-and-fifty guests and the cake you brought is only big enough for *maybe* seventy-five!" she frantically told me.

"Oh no! How can that be?" I said. "I baked and prepared the cake to the specifications on the invoice!" So I asked, "What time will they be serving the cake?" Thank goodness it was not to be cut and served for about five hours from then.

"OK, let me make it right! I'll be back before the cake cutting with enough sheet cakes to make up the difference. That way, all guests will get cake at least," I assured her.

I couldn't freaking believe this! How could this have happened? A giant pit filled my stomach as I realized my mistake. No groom's cake—fine—but I had neglected to increase the size of the bridal cake to make up for it.

I baked, blast chilled, and frosted sheet cakes like a maniac. I rushed back to the venue in plenty of time for the catering staff to cut and serve the cake.

Disaster averted, right? Or so I thought.

The following day, I reached out to the mother of the bride to sincerely apologize for my mistake and to thank her for letting me "make it right." She wouldn't take my call and instead sent me a strongly worded email about how I "ruined her daughter's wedding" and how they didn't even do the cake cutting ceremony because she was so upset about the "small" wedding cake. She even demanded a full refund!

I felt so horrible that I didn't take another wedding cake order for months.

Even though I didn't end up giving her a refund—they had cut, served, and consumed the entirety of the cake I brought—to this day, I still remember it as a learning experience for myself.

I had provided customer service but not to the best of my ability. Since then, I make sure that one of my customer service steps with every single order is to make sure that there is a service agreement and notes kept in my bakery software so that when I go to actually prepare the cake, I am certain to catch everything!

Customer service is just as important to your cake and baking business as the product itself. This is the area in your business where you really have a chance to shine and show them that it's not "just a cake." You are creating so much more than that! It's the entire experience, and not just on the day of the event. You have the opportunity to put them at ease by delivering an amazing experience from the day they ask for the quote to the week after they've enjoyed your delicious artistic creation.

Since I started focusing more on the customer experience, my business has grown by word-of-mouth from happy customers as well as from my own marketing efforts.

Along with the straight business tips I'm going to share, I also want to share my "secret superpower" that I use to make the whole cake order process easy and fun for my customers.

Are you ready to hear what it is? It's asking your customers lots of questions and then *listening*.

Remember, you are solving a problem for them. Customers need to know that you are supporting them for their special event. They also want to know that you will create a delicious and memorable dessert that their guests will talk about for years to come!

One of my favorite experiences, after I've done a cake for someone, is hearing from them even years later about how much they loved a cake I created and how they still talk about those special little details that I captured. You want your customers to look back on their event and experience the joy all over again.

Here are some tips that can help your customers have a great experience every step of the way:

Terms and Conditions: Every business should have a solid set of Terms and Conditions, and in a baking business (especially a home-based one), this is a must! Included below and in the book's resources section is a basic Terms and Conditions template that you are welcome to modify to fit your own business needs.

Note: The information contained within this template is provided as a guideline only and is not intended as a substitute for obtaining legal, accounting, tax, or other financial advice from your professional counsel. Presentation of the information via the Internet is not intended to create, and receipt does not constitute, a legal/accounting-client relationship. Users of this template are advised to consult your own legal counsel for further information relevant to your own business location.

DISCLAIMER of WARRANTIES and LIMITATIONS of LIABILITY

This template is provided on an "as is" and "as available" basis. Use of this template is at your own risk. We and our suppliers disclaim all warranties. Neither we nor our suppliers shall be liable for any damages of any kind due to the use of this template.

I like to describe Terms and Conditions as a document that states the expectations and makes sure that you and your customer are both on the same page. Here is an example of a basic Terms and Conditions document:

TERMS AND CONDITIONS

All Products made by [YOUR BUSINESS NAME HERE] are subject to the following Terms and Conditions.

INGREDIENTS

All products are produced according to the Cottage Foods Act [OR your area's governing authority] in the State of [INSERT YOUR STATE OR THE REGION WHERE YOU CONDUCT BUSINESS] and may contain or come into contact with soy, wheat, dairy, nuts, or other allergens. These products are not intended for resale.

It is the responsibility of the Customer to inform [YOUR BUSINESS NAME HERE], prior to the confirmation of their booking, of any allergy/intolerance issues. It is the responsibility of the Customer to inform their guests of all allergy/intolerance information, and accordingly, the Supplier will not be held liable for any allergic reaction resulting from consumption of the cake.

All special dietary products are NOT guaranteed suitable for allergies and are suitable for intolerances only.

All products are made to be eaten on the day of the celebration.

QUOTATIONS

All Quotations are valid for five days from the date of issue.

In the event that the desired date has been filled by another order/customer, prior to the Customer confirming the booking, [YOUR BUSINESS NAME HERE] is not obliged to honor the quote.

All Quotations are not bookings. All Quotations are subject to availability.

ORDERS

Here at [YOUR BUSINESS NAME HERE], we prefer at least thirty (30) days notice for all orders, as we are continually booked in advance. We will, however, endeavor, where availability permits, to accept short-notice cakes.

Any Products ordered from a picture or photo of a product produced by any other cake maker can only be reproduced by [YOUR BUSINESS NAME HERE] as our interpretation of that product and will NOT be an exact reproduction of the product in the picture or photo.

DEPOSITS

A non-refundable deposit of 50 percent is required to hold your date within fourteen (14) days prior to pickup or delivery. (Wedding cake orders are subject to separate deposit terms: a non-refundable deposit of $250 due at the booking of wedding cake order).

If [YOUR BUSINESS NAME HERE] has delivered a product that is an accurate interpretation of what has been quoted and invoiced but the Customer does not accept the finished Product, the deposit WILL NOT be refunded. The Customer can choose to pay the remainder and take the Product/s, or leave them at no extra cost.

If an order is placed within (7) days prior to pick up, a 75 percent deposit is expected within twenty-four hours of invoice. If order placed within three (3) days prior to pickup, payment in full is required and due upon receipt.

UNFORESEEN CIRCUMSTANCES

Where [YOUR BUSINESS NAME HERE] cancels the booking due to illness or any other unforeseen circumstance that affects the ability to deliver the ordered Product, the deposit will be refunded within seven (7) days of notification to the Customer.

The deposit will be refunded via bank transfer only, and the Customer will need to provide these bank details to [YOUR BUSINESS NAME HERE].

FINAL BALANCE PAYMENTS AND PICKUPS

The balance is due on or before the pickup or delivery date, and before the Product or delivery personnel leaves the premises. (Wedding cake balances are due ten (10) days PRIOR to wedding date).

If paying by cash, correct change is appreciated, as no cash is kept on the premises. Change will not be able to be provided by [YOUR BUSINESS NAME HERE].

If paying by internet transfer (i.e., Zelle, PayPal, or Venmo), the money needs to clear into the account BEFORE the product or delivery personnel leaves the premises.

If an order is placed within the seven (7) days prior to pick up, a 75 percent deposit is expected within twenty-four hours of the invoice.

DELIVERY

Delivery will be carried out in a safe and appropriate manner. Once delivered to the customer and change of hands has been completed with the product in appropriate condition, it is then up to the Customer to store and care for the cake as per [YOUR BUSINESS NAME HERE]'s instructions. If anything is to happen to the cake after this exchange and deemed to be the fault of the Customer through not following the instructions provided, [YOUR BUSINESS NAME HERE] is not liable for any damages.

A delivery date and time will be agreed upon by both parties, and if the Customer is not at the location at this time and date, and [YOUR BUSINESS NAME HERE] is not able to contact the Customer, the product will be transported back with [YOUR BUSINESS NAME HERE] and it will be the Customer's responsibility to collect the product at a time that suits [YOUR BUSINESS NAME HERE].

PUBLICATION

[YOUR BUSINESS NAME HERE] reserves the right to use any image of a Product made by us for publication at a later date.

[YOUR BUSINESS NAME HERE] will endeavor to not post any photos on social media or other platforms until after your event has taken place.

[YOUR BUSINESS NAME HERE] will never use any image that is supplied by the Customer, without first obtaining the Customer's permission (i.e., children's birthday parties and photos of the events).

RETURN OF RENTED EQUIPMENT

Deposits are taken for all equipment. All equipment must be returned on the agreed date or extra charges may be levied to cover hire costs. Any damages to equipment will incur a reduction of deposit returned in order to cover costs of repair or replacement.

Equipment rental price, deposit, and all other charges will vary depending on which item of equipment is being rented and in what condition and time frame it is returned by the Customer.

GIFT VOUCHERS

Any gift vouchers or flyers being redeemed will only be honored if the pickup/delivery date is within the expiration period of the voucher.

The voucher or flyer must be presented upon picking up baked goods, otherwise, the items cannot leave the premises. The voucher must be surrendered upon pickup of baked goods as it will be treated like cash.

DAMAGE

It is the responsibility of the Customer to check the state of the product before leaving the premises. Once the item has left the premises, the Customer has accepted the item as is and is responsible for ensuring that product(s) gets to its destination safely and is stored as per instructions from [YOUR BUSINESS NAME HERE] to achieve best results for taste and quality and to avoid any damage.

Other considerations are:

1. THIRD PARTY PICKUP

If a third party will be collecting the cake on the Customer's behalf, this party will be given all appropriate information that would have been given to the customer. Same conditions apply as if the customer were to collect themselves.

2. SERVING SIZES

Standard serves are based on a size of 2" x 2" x 3" or 4" high. Cake serving sizes are estimated. Specialty cakes, carved cakes, and the method of slicing may affect the ultimate serving number. The Customer understands and accepts these terms and must order their products accordingly after having considered these variables.

3. POSTPONEMENT

If for any reason the event is required to be post-poned, please contact me immediately.

The new date proposed will be subject to availability.

4.   CANCELLATIONS/REFUNDS

If cancellation of the order is required and you have paid your full balance, the refund policy is as follows:

I If the cancellation is up to one (1) month in advance of your event date, you will receive a refund, less your initial deposit and the cost of any supplies already purchased for your cake.

II) If the cancellation is less than seven (7) days prior to your event, there will be absolutely no refunds given.

III) Refunds will be paid within thirty (30) days of cancellation.

IV) The monies, if owed, will be refunded via bank transfer only, and the Customer will need to provide these bank details to [YOUR BUSINESS NAME HERE].

Please note: Any non-refunded balance may be credited toward future purchases at the discretion of [YOUR BUSINESS NAME HERE].

All Terms and Conditions subject to change.

Customer Service Lifecycle: The steps from getting the cake request to the final delivery

F irst contact: When a potential customer reaches out for a quote, respond quickly and professionally. If you can't give a quote quickly, at least respond to let them know when you will get back to them.

Quoting: If you are available on the date, generate a quote and get it to them quickly (usually same-day or next-day). If you are unable to generate the quote immediately, respond to their request as soon as you can to let them know you will get back to them.

Follow up after the quote: Give the customer twenty-four to forty-eight hours then follow up if you haven't heard back. People get busy and they appreciate a reminder. It's easy to say something like this, "Hi! I'm following up to make sure you received the quote I sent and to see if there are any questions that I can answer for you?" That way you stay on top of the situation but you're doing so in a way that is helpful to the customer.

Getting the order/invoice: If the customer decides to book the order with you, then you will convert the quote to an invoice and ask for the deposit. Collecting a deposit is crucial! It's common practice and shows that you are a professional and your time is important. It also ensures that your customers are serious and cuts down on cancellations and other problems.

Reminder for deposit: Each week you should go through your upcoming orders and make sure that everyone has paid their deposit on time. If you find someone who hasn't paid the deposit, send them a friendly deposit reminder with the invoice and let them know that their order is not secure until you receive the deposit. Again, people get busy and they may have just forgotten and will appreciate you helping them stay on track .

A few days before pickup or delivery: I always reach out to the customer a few days or even the week before their cake order just to let them know that I have everything on track and that I will be touching base with them a few days prior to pick up or delivery. Again, this is just a courtesy so that they know you haven't forgotten about them and that you're excited to create something amazing for their celebration.

A day or two before pick up or delivery: I usually will send a quick message by text to touch base again and let them know that I'm confirming the final details on delivery or pickup to make sure that we're all on the same page.

The day of pickup or delivery: Dress profession-ally (I wear a chef's coat or apron), or if you have another branded shirt or uniform, that works too, so long as you look clean and nice and have a smile on your face! I also always include a cutting and serving guide. Customers not only appreciate this, but it helps ensure that they received the number of servings for which they paid. This will help cover you in the event that they claim they didn't get enough cake when really they just cut the pieces too big!

If they are picking up the cake from you, make sure that you help them to their car and set them up for transporting the cake.

After the delivery or pickup: I always take photographs of my cakes in my studio with my nice camera and good photo backdrops. I love to send the client a thank-you card with a picture of their cake thanking them for the order and for their business and wishing them well. I use an online software application called sendoutcards.com (there are other online applications that do the same thing) where you can upload photos and they will print the photos on custom greeting cards for you and send it to your recipient. The point is to make sure you send a personalized thank-you card. I know from experience that my customers absolutely love getting a thank-you card, especially with a picture of their cake!

Getting Repeat Customers

Besides providing excellent customer service through the whole cycle of their first cake order, there are things that you can do to increase the chances that they will become a repeat customer:

- Keep a calendar of customer events like wedding dates, birthdays, etc. and send emails or text messages to those customers a few months before each event comes up on the calendar the next year.

- Did a wedding cake last year? Send them a happy anniversary card, text, or email and ask if they would like a quote on an anniversary cake.

- Use the same method for birthdays! Offer a free quote for the upcoming birthday. A lot of times people really do appreciate this. I've had many customers tell me, "Thank goodness you do this! I would have totally forgotten to get on your calendar and then I would have been sad that I couldn't have your cake!"

Here are some other things you can do to provide great customer service:

- Be confident and smile! (Do this even when you're on the phone—it will come across in your tone.)

- Be clear and concise in your communication. If there is a problem, be professional but firm in the resolution.

- Make sure your customers know how to get ahold of you and when they can expect a reply.

- Guide your customer in choosing the right cake for *them*.

- Remember, they are the hero of the story.

- Ask for an honest review and get their permission to share it!

Cake-tastic

Remember my wedding disaster story at the beginning of the chapter? I've grown and improved tons since then, but things still can and *will* "go wrong." I had a very unique wedding cake just this past year. The couple wanted a nature-inspired cake with edible moss as they love hiking and the mountains. I designed a hyper-realistic cake that looked like a tree stump with turkey tail mushrooms, bark, and moss.

When I delivered the cake, the couple was able to see it and everyone was so surprised and stunned. They loved it!

I set it up on the cake table, and as is my normal practice, I provided the catering staff with the cutting guide to ensure that they would know how to serve it properly for the number of guests.

The next day, I got a call from the groom's mother telling me how wonderful the cake was, except for one thing. *Oh God, what?* I thought to myself. Apparently, the catering staff did not follow my cutting guide and they served giant pieces to the first guests and then the pieces got increasingly smaller as they realized that there was not going to be enough! The bride and groom didn't even get any!

I felt so terrible for them! They were so excited! The mother of the groom assured me that they were not upset with me but with the venue staff.

"Oh, this is not OK!" I assured her. I would make this right.

So, I re-created the wedding cake, design and all, in a miniature version and delivered it to the couple's home at no charge.

They were so surprised and happy! I received the most amazing heartfelt thank-you card ever.

That's how you can provide great customer service!

Chapter Eight

Next Steps and Additional Resources

> *"You miss one hundred percent of the shots you don't take." —Wayne Gretzky*

Cake-tastrophe

I spent years of my adult life wishing I had my own baking business, but my reality was getting up every day and going to work in an office. Sure, I was doing something that I was good at, and it paid the bills. While I didn't exactly hate my job, I didn't feel fulfilled either, and I certainly lacked a passion for it. There were days when it felt truly soul-crushing, and the clock seemed to move so slowly!

Many times each day I would peel my eyes away from the huge pile of papers and folders on my desk and I would look around thinking to myself, "Ugh. I'm at work right now."

It didn't happen overnight, but I never lost sight of my passion for cake art and design.

Cake-tastic

Taking the leap to live my sweet business dream has been the greatest decision of my life! Now my reality is filled with my passion for baking, and I get to bring joy to others, one bite at a time.

Every so often when I'm in my studio working on a cake, I pause, look around at how far I've come, and say to myself with complete joy, "Hell yeah! I'm at work right now!"

My hope is that you will do the same. As I shared at the beginning of our journey together, I've dreamt of living my sweet business dream my whole life, and now that I have achieved that dream, every day gets better and better.

I think about how many people I've brought joy to with my creations. I reflect on how many events I've been a sweet part of and how I'm fulfilling what I believe to be my life's purpose. I know that might sound silly to others: "Your life's purpose is making cakes?" To this, I say, "Yes! And so much more! I bring happiness and help others create memories and epic experiences."

I believe that everyone has a special gift to share with the world, and if you've had the dream as I have, then it's no accident that we've met and that I got to share my story with you so you too can say with joy, "Hell yeah! I'm at work right now!"

So what are your next steps? I invite you to believe in yourself and go forth and make your dream your reality! Take it one step at a time, and if you need more help, I'm here for you. Ask me questions and share your wins and struggles with me—I really do want to hear about your journey!

And if you want more support, here are some other ways we can work together:

Join Cake Biz Bootcamp: This is my signature subscription-based online course. It includes work-books and video tutorial lessons, plus personalized guidance to help you no matter where you are in your baking business journey. Visit https://cakebi-zbootcamp.com/ for more information.

Join my private Facebook group:

Click here to request to join: https://www.facebook.com/groups/1676196029272616

In this group, you can follow along with baking business tips, cake, and baking resources, and even ask baking-related questions. There are thousands of members from all over the world.

Read my blog: Visit https://angelfoods.net/ for free resources and recipes.

Listen to my podcast, *The Cake Biz Broadcast: Sweet Snippets for Success*. I share frequent business tips for bakers, and I interview top baking industry leaders who share their stories. Visit https://thecakebiz-broadcast.libsyn.com/ to listen, rate, and subscribe.

Follow me on social media for pictures of my cakes and more business tips:

https://www.facebook.com/cakebusinessschool

https://www.facebook.com/snarkysweetcakechick

https://www.instagram.com/cakebusinessschoolllc/

https://www.pinterest.com/angelfoods

https://www.youtube.com/channel/UCqAUCprXWI70--ecqpeIVzg

Subscribe to my YouTube channel:
https://youtube.com/@cakebusinessschoolllc

Other Resources:

Software:

Convertkit: This is **a full-featured email service provider** (ESP). Thanks to its ease of use, automation, and other features, it's one of the fastest-growing email marketing companies around. It also offers customizable sign-up forms and landing pages to help bring in more email subscribers. Visit my affiliate link for a free 14 day trial: https://convertkit.com/?lmref=hbDgQA

BiziChix: This is a service for a quick and easy website set up for your cake or baking business. Visit my affiliate link for more information here: https://bizichix.com/?bca=2

BakeDiary : BakeDiary is the leading cloud-based software for cake decorators and bakers all over the world to help manage the admin side of your cake business. Visit this link to sign up: https://www.bakediary.com/

Recommended Reads:

By Mike Michalowicz:

> *Profit First: Transform Your Business from a Cash-Eating Monster to a Money-Making Machine*

> *The Pumpkin Plan: A Simple Strategy to Grow a Remarkable Business in Any Field*

> *Get Different: Marketing That Can't Be Ignored!*

By Donald Miller:

> *Building a Story Brand: Clarify Your Message So Customers Will Listen*

By Denise Duffield Thomas:

> *Get Rich Lucky Bitch!*

> *Chill and Prosper: The New Way to Grow Your Business, Make Millions, and Change the World*

Acknowledgments

I'd like to thank the following people who cheered me on while writing this book:

My husband, Jeff, who has been my biggest supporter and cheerleader in this journey.

My favorite business author, Mike Michalowicz, who inspired me to write.

My Cake Business Coach, Rebekah, who coached me through the process of pursuing my cake passion full time.

My Soul Coach, Stephanie, who helped me with my confidence and mindset.

My book support team, Jordan, Shelby, Patti, Kerk, and all the amazing people at Self Publishing School, who helped with every step of the writing process.

And last, but certainly not least, my family and friends who have always been so gracious to listen to my rambling about all things cake!

Author Bio:

A former Accountant, Nicole Bendig-Lamb successfully turned her hobby of baking into a full-time gig as the owner of Snarky Sweet Cake Chick, LLC. She helps her clients create epic memories for their celebrations as a Master Cake Designer and Former Food Network Competitor. She also owns and operates Cake Business School, LLC where she educates and coaches other hobby & home-based bakers on the business side of baking. As a Certified Profit First Professional and Certified Fix This Next Advisor, she's got the skills and experience to help you with your sweet business dreams!

Can I Ask for Your Help?

Did you love this book? Don't forget to leave a review!

Every review matters, and it matters a *lot!*

I invite you to head over to Amazon or wherever you purchased this book to leave an honest review for me. This helps me make the next version of this book and future books even better:

Bakingyourwaytothetop.com/review

I appreciate your support!

–Nicole